This book is a

Gift

From
....

To
....

Date
....

May God bless you through this book

Prayers for breakthrough in your business

PRAYERS FOR BREAKTHROUGH IN YOUR BUSINESS

PRAYERS FOR BREAKTHROUGH IN YOUR BUSINESS

Copyright © 2014

PRAYER M. MADUEKE

ISBN:

Prayer Publications

All rights reserved. No part of this work may be reproduced or transmitted in any form or by any means without written permission from the publisher

Unless otherwise indicated, all Scripture quotations are taken from the King James Version of the Bible, and used by permission. All emphasis within quotations is the author's additions.

First Edition, 2014

For further information of permission

1 Babatunde close, off Olaitan Street, Surulere, Lagos, Nigeria
+234 803 353 0599
Email: pastor@prayermadueke.com,
Website: www.prayermadueke.com

Dedication

This book is dedicated to people who are trusting God to achieve success in their businesses and careers. The Lord who sees your sincere dedication will answer your prayers Amen.

Prayers for breakthrough in your business

BOOK OVERVIEW

PRAYERS FOR BREAKTHROUGH IN YOUR BUSINESS

- *Business breakthrough is very important*
- *Attacks on businesses from evil altars*
- *Hijacked business breakthrough*

BUSINESS BREAKTHROUGH IS VERY IMPORTANT

Every good businessperson understands what it means to experience breakthrough in business. Without this experience, the business would die naturally. While God wants you to prosper in your business, your enemy, the devil, does not want you to prosper. He wants you to fail.

That is why devil has stationed the forces of darkness in diverse places to stop people's businesses from moving forward. You could have been destined to succeed in your field of business but when you fail to deal with the forces of darkness, it would be so hard for you to make it no matter how much you try.

> *"And there came an angel of the LORD, and sat under an oak which was in Ophrah, that pertained unto Josh the Abi–ezrite: and his son Gideon threshed wheat by the winepress, to hide it from the Midianites. And the angel of the LORD appeared unto him, and said unto him, The LORD is with thee, thou mighty man of valor. And Gideon said unto him, Oh my Lord, if the LORD were with us, why then is all this befallen us. In addition, where be all his miracles, which our fathers told us of, saying, did not the LORD bring us up from Egypt? Now the LORD hath forsaken us, and delivered us into the hands of the Midianites. And the LORD looked upon him, and said, Go in this thy might, and thou shalt save Israel from the hand of the Midianites: have not I sent thee? And he said unto him, Oh my Lord, wherewith shall I save Israel? Behold, my family is poor in Manasseh, and I am the least in my father's house"* (Judges 6:11-15).

Gideon was defeated in his life by these forces. In his father's farmland, these forces occupied the place to enjoy their harvests. These powers influenced the Midianites to oppress Gideon and his people. Gideon was thrashing his father's wheat in his father's farm to hide it from the Midianites.

They cultivated the ground and planted but the Midianites enjoy their harvest. While they suffered, their enemies enjoyed their increase and harvest. It was a sad situation.

There are people today who do businesses with people's destinies. People work hard but do not get rewards for their efforts. This is not right. The devil labors to contradict God's Word and to make it invalid. God said that a man would reap what he sowed, but the devil is saying that another man would reap what you sowed. Unfortunately, that is what is happening with the businesses of many people today.

> *"Be not deceived; God is not mocked: for whatsoever a man sowed, that shall he also reap. For he that sowed to his flesh shall of the flesh reap corruption; but he that sowed to the Spirit shall of the Spirit reap life everlasting"* (Galatians 6:7-8).

> *"And it came to pass, as we went to prayer, a certain damsel possessed with a spirit of divination met us, which brought her masters much gain by soothsaying: The same followed Paul and us, and cried, saying, These men are the servants of the most high God, which shew unto us the way of salvation. And this did her many days. However, Paul, being grieved, turned and said to the spirit, I command thee in the name of Jesus Christ to come out of her. In addition, he*

> *came out the same hour. And when her masters saw that the hope of their gains was gone, they caught Paul and Silas, and drew them into the marketplace unto the rulers"* (Acts 16:16-19).

The bible had a story of a young girl that went through this kind of problem. This damsel had so much strength and power to labor. She had all that it takes to succeed, make great profit and live comfortably well to help herself and others. The devil saw this and inspired some people to invoke an evil spirit to possess her.

The duty of that evil spirit was not to reduce her strength, energy and talent but to divert all her gains to the satanic kingdom for his agents to make much gain. This kind of spirit is very wicked. This is not the spirit of premature death, sickness or weakness. It is a spirit that helps you to do more work for evil men to enjoy your labor. It is a spirit that allows people to labor and suffer, and empowers satanic agents to enjoy your harvest.

This wicked spirit possessed this young girl for many years. Her talent was employed to profit wicked people while she suffered and moved about like a mad person. She was a diviner who made much gain for her masters through soothsaying. She encountered Paul's evangelistic team and said correct things about them but Paul was grieved and he cast out the spirit that possessed her. Paul delivered her and set her free while the occult grandmasters began to record losses in their evil businesses of soul trading and destiny amputation.

> *"And build an altar unto the LORD thy God upon the top of this rock, in the ordered place, and take the second bullock, and offer a burnt sacrifice with the wood of the grove which thou shall cut*

down. Then Gideon took ten men of his servants, and did as the LORD had said unto him: and so it was, because he feared his father's household, and the men of the city, that he could not do it by day, that he did it by night" (Judges 6:26-27).

The case of Gideon was similar to that of this young girl. He planted threshed wheat but the Midianites came and took them all. His problem was physical but the young girl's was spiritual. Most of our battles today are more spiritual than physical. A great battle is going on between God's children and Satan's agents.

"For we wrestle not against flesh and blood, but against principalities, against powers, against the rulers of the darkness of this world, against spiritual wickedness in high places" (Ephesians 6:12).

"For though we walk in the flesh, we do not war after the flesh: (For the weapons of our warfare are not carnal, but mighty through God to the pulling down of strong holds;) Casting down imaginations, and every high thing that exalted itself against the knowledge of God, and bringing into captivity every thought to the obedience of Christ" (2 Corinthians 10:3-5).

Many people are already defeated and the result is what you see everywhere. Many business people today are not making it because of devil's agents who know how to divert their gains to make much profit. You need to start praying and asking God to reveal the cause of your problems.

ATTACKS ON BUSINESSES FROM EVIL ALTARS

Many Christians are yet to come to the knowledge of the reality of evil altars. An altar is raised, typically flat-topped, structure or area where spiritual ceremonies are performed. Principally, satanic agents, including witches and wizards, erect altars where they gather to carry out their activities and evil plans.

When satanic agents want to afflict people, they use their evil altars. When they want to waste people's progress, they use evil altars. When they want to oppress people's stars, they use evil altars. When they want to capture anointing on people's lives, they use evil altars. When they want to limit people's lives, they use evil altars. When they want to frustrate plans, they use evil altars. When they want to kill people and bury them while such people still live, they use evil altars. When they want to place a curse on someone's business, they use evil altars. When they want to place yokes of limitation on people's efforts, they use evil altars.

When they want to control people against God's will, they use evil altars. When they want to impose satanic fear on people, they use evil altars. When they want to useless someone's effort, they use evil altars. When they want to send evil forces to someone's business, they use evil altars. When they want good things to abandon someone, they use evil altars. When they want people to be tired of life, they use evil altars. When they want to arrest a promising star, they use evil altars. When they want people to live wasted lives, they use evil altars. When they want to announce people's failures, they use evil altars. When they want to summon people for evil, they use evil altars. When they want to cause confusion in any life, place or thing, they use evil altars. When they want to have access to people's health, they use evil altars. When they want to remove someone from an exalted position, they use evil altars.

When they want to eat human flesh and drink people's blood, they use evil altars. When they want to do evil transfer, they use evil altars. When they want to behead important heads, they use evil altars. When satanic agents want to fellowship with the devil, they use evil altars. When they want to introduce evil on earth, they use evil altars. When they want to block people's access to favor, they use evil altars. When they want to break marriages, they use evil altars. When they want to raise enemies, they use evil altars. Do you still doubt the activities of evil agents?

> *"^{1}And Balaam said unto Balak, Build me here seven altars, and prepare me here seven oxen and seven rams. ^{2}And Balak did as Balaam had spoken; and Balak and Balaam offered on every altar a bullock and a ram. ^{3}And Balaam said unto Balak, Stand by thy burnt offering, and I will go: peradventure the LORD will come to meet me: and whatsoever he showed me I would tell thee. In addition, he went to a high place. ^{13}And Balak said unto him, Come, I pray thee, with me unto another place, from whence thou mayest see them: thou shall see but the utmost part of them, and shall not see them all: and curse me them from thence. ^{14}And he brought him into the field of Zophim, to the top of Pisgah, and built seven altars, and offered a bullock and a ram on every altar"* (Numbers 23:1-3, 13-14).

King Balak once invited Balaam to kill the people of God and stop their journey to the Promised Land. To achieve their aim, they decided to build altars, have fellowship with the devil and mobilize evil spirits to kill the children of Israel. When they failed in the first seven altars, they decided to build another seven altars where they would curse them.

> *"And Balak said unto Balaam, Come, I pray thee, I will bring thee unto another place; peradventure it will please God that thou mayest curse me them from thence. And Balak brought Balaam unto the top of Peor that looked toward Jeshimon. And Balaam said unto Balak, Build me here seven altars, and prepare me here seven bullocks and seven rams. And Balak did as Balaam had said, and offered a bullock and a ram on every altar"* (Numbers 23:27-30).

When they built another seven altars to the children of Israel, they still failed. When they investigated, they found out that their enchantments and divinations failed because God did not see iniquity in the camp of God's children. As a result, the people of God were united and God was with them.

> *"[21]He hath not beheld iniquity in Jacob neither hath he seen perverseness in Israel: the LORD his God is with him and the shout of a king is among them. [23]Surely there is no enchantment against Jacob, neither is there any divination against Israel: according to this time it shall be said of Jacob and of Israel, What hath God wrought"* (Numbers 23:21, 23).

With the erection of 21 evil altars, they planned to bring iniquity to their camp. They raised agents of perversion, fired arrows of immorality and disobedience to the elders and the Word of God. They raised wayward women to seduce the children of Israel.

> "^{1}And Israel abode in Shittim and the people began to commit whoredom with the daughters of Moab. ^{2}And they called the people unto the sacrifices of their gods: and the people did eat, and bowed down to their gods. ^{3}And Israel joined himself unto Baal–peor: and the anger of the LORD was kindled against Israel. ^{9}And those that died in the plague were twenty and four thousand" (Numbers 25:1-3, 9).

Evil altars are places evil agents offer sacrifices to discover the power that holds God's children. It a place they enquire for people's destinies in order to destroy them. They discover the secret plans of God for a person or place at their alter.

> "^{6}And he returned unto him, and, lo, he stood by his burnt sacrifice, he, and all the princes of Moab. ^{17}And when he came to him, behold, he stood by his burnt offering, and the princes of Moab with him. And Balak said unto him, what hath the LORD spoken?" (Numbers 23: 6, 17).

It is a place where Gideon's breakthrough, destiny and progress were arrested.

HIJACKED BUSINESS BREAKTHROUGH

Having seen how evil agents could use evil altars to inquire about people's businesses, there is no doubt that these wicked agents have captured many people's business breakthroughs. That is why many people struggle so much and cannot give accounts of their efforts.

Satan visited Adam and Eve in form of a serpent. He convinced and influenced them to eat the forbidden fruit, which God commanded them not to eat. In so doing, devil captured their destiny.

> *"Now the serpent was more subtle than any beast of the field which the LORD God had made. In addition, he said unto the woman, Yea, hath God said, ye shall not eat of every tree of the garden? And the woman said unto the serpent, we may eat of the fruit of the trees of the garden: But of the fruit of the tree, which is in the midst of the garden, God, hath said, Ye shall not eat of it, neither shall ye touch it, lest ye die. And the serpent said unto the woman, Ye shall not surely die: ⁵For God doth know that in the day ye eat thereof, then your eyes shall be opened, and ye shall be as gods, knowing good and evil. And when the woman saw that the tree* was *good for food, and that it* was *pleasant to the eyes, and a tree to be desired to make* one *wise, she took of the fruit thereof, and did eat, and gave also unto her husband with her; and he did eat"* (Genesis 3:1-6).

When you disobey the written Word of God and fail to repent, restitute and forsake such sins, devil will arrest your breakthrough. When Adam disobeyed God, He cursed him and drove him out of his inheritance, which was his place of comfort. His soil, which was the place of business, was cursed and sorrow replaced his joy. Thorns and thistles entered his business and he began to sweat and till the ground to produce what to eat.

Furthermore, when Cain killed his brother, Abel, his family became bloody. The blood of Abel cried against Cain's breakthrough. God also cursed him and he became a vagabond and the first fugitive on earth.

> *"⁵But if thou wilt not send him, we will not go down: for the man said unto us, ye shall not see my face, except your brother be with you. ⁶And Israel said, Wherefore dealt ye so ill with me, as to tell the man whether ye had yet a brother? ⁷And they said, The man asked us strictly of our state, and of our kindred, saying, Is your father yet alive? Have ye another brother? In addition, we told him according to the tenor of these words: could we certainly know that he would say, bring your brother down. ⁸And Judah said unto Israel his father, Send the lad with me, and we will arise and go; that we may live, and not die, both we, and thou, and our little ones. ⁹I will be surety for him; of my hand shalt thou require him: if I bring him not unto thee, and set him before thee, then let me bear the blame for ever: ¹¹And their father Israel said unto them, If it must be so now, do this; take of the best fruits in the land in your vessels, and carry down the man a present, a little balm, and a little honey, spices, and myrrh, nuts, and almonds: ¹²And take double money in your hand; and the money that was brought again in the mouth of your sacks, carry it again in your hand; peradventure it was an oversight"* (Genesis 43:5-9, 11-12).

When you commit abortion or shed innocent blood, it will affect anything you do on earth. The blood that you shed would cry against you year after year. When you come from a bloody foundation, the same thing will happen to you. Devil has arrested many businesses because of their disobedience, blood crying against them and all manner of sins.

God asked Gideon to do something before his arrested destiny was released. He told David, I do not have problems with you. Yet, David's government was affected because he inherited the throne from a bloody man.

> *"¹Then there was a famine in the days of David three years, year after year; and David enquired of the LORD. In addition, the LORD answered, it is for Saul, and for his bloody house, because he slew the Gibeonites. ³Wherefore David said unto the Gibeonites, What should I do for you? And wherewith shall I make the atonement, which ye may bless, the inheritance of the LORD?"* (2 Samuel 21:1, 3).

The people that are supposed to inherit good things from the Lord were in famine because the blood that cried against them polluted their foundation. Your business may be passing through many problems now because of the root of your family. That is why you need to find out the history of your great grandparents.

The breakthrough and investment that Lot had was destroyed in Sodom because he invested in a wrong place. You need to check where your business is located. The location of your business could be the reason why your breakthrough is under arrest.

> *"The word of the LORD came also unto me, saying, Thou shall not take thee a wife, neither shall thou have sons or daughters in this place. For thus saith the LORD concerning the sons and concerning the daughters that are born in this place, and concerning their mothers that bare them, and concerning their fathers that begat them in this land; They shall die of grievous deaths; they shall not be lamented; neither shall they be buried; but they shall be as dung upon the face of the earth: and they shall be consumed by the sword, and by famine; and their carcasses shall be meat for the fowls of heaven, and for the beasts of the earth"* (Jeremiah 16:1-4).

Dinah, the virgin daughter of Jacob, visited a wrong place and she lost her virginity and destiny. Reuben slept with his father's concubine, Bilhab, and his destiny and that of his children unborn were arrested.

> *"^{22}And it came to pass, when Israel dwelt in that land, that Reuben went and lay with Bilhah his father's concubine: and Israel heard it. Now the sons of Jacob were twelve: ^{3}Reuben, thou art my firstborn, my might, and the beginning of my strength, the Excellency of dignity, and the excellence of power: ^{4}Unstable as water, thou shall not excel; because thou wentest up to thy father's bed; then defiledst thou it: he went up to my couch"* (Genesis 35:22; 49:3-4).

Do you know why your businesses have refused to move forward? Do you know what your ancestors did? Do you know what gods or evil altars your father worshipped? God told Gideon to deal with his father's idol before he could move forward. When he obeyed God, his blessings came. Do you see why it is important to deal with your family's idols?

> "²⁵And it came to pass the same night, that the LORD said unto him, Take thy father's young bullock, even the second bullock of seven years old, and throw down the altar of Baal that thy father hath, and cut down the grove that is by it: ²⁶And build an altar unto the LORD thy God upon the top of this rock, in the ordered place, and take the second bullock, and offer a burnt sacrifice with the wood of the grove which thou shall cut down. ²⁷Then Gideon took ten men of his servants, and did as the LORD had said unto him: and so it was, because he feared his father's household, and the men of the city, that he could not do it by day, that he did it by night. ²⁴And Gideon sent messengers throughout all mount Ephraim, saying, Come down against the Midianites, and take before them the waters unto Beth–barah and Jordan. Then all the men of Ephraim gathered themselves together, and took the waters unto Beth–barah and Jordan. ²⁵And they took two princes of the Midianites, Oreb and Zeeb; and they slew Oreb upon the rock Oreb, and Zeeb they slew at the winepress of Zeeb, and pursued Midian, and brought the heads of Oreb and Zeeb to Gideon on the other side Jordan" (Judges 6:25-27; 7:24-25).

If you would undo evil your fathers have done, your business would be set free and released from captivity. Achan stole an accursed thing; a Babylonian garment and all the members of his family died as a result. He lost his life, household and made Israel to suffer defeat in war. Samson chose a wife, who was a harlot, by sight. He really loved Delilah but at the end, he lost his anointing, his eyes and his life.

> "¹Then went Samson to Gaza, and saw there a harlot, and went in unto her. ⁴And it happened

afterward, that he loved a woman in the valley of Sorek, whose name was Delilah. ⁵And the lords of the Philistines came up unto her, and said unto her, Entice him, and see wherein his great strength lieth, and by what means we may prevail against him, that we may bind him to afflict him: and we will give thee every one of us eleven hundred pieces of silver. ⁶And Delilah said to Samson, Tell me, I pray thee, wherein thy great strength lieth, and wherewith thou mightest be bound to afflict thee. ⁷And Samson said unto her, If they bind me with seven green withs that were never dried, then shall I be weak, and be as another man. ²⁰And she said, The Philistines be upon thee, Samson. In addition, he awoke out of his sleep, and said, I will go out as at other times before, and shake myself. And he wist not that the LORD was departed from him" (Judges 16:1, 4-7, 20).

Your business cannot suffer ordinarily. Find out why your business is suffering setbacks and ask God to show you what to do about it and you will prevail over financial crisis and have business breakthrough. Many business people started very well in life. They used to be very prosperous in business, but today, they eat from hand to mouth. Some others are watching their businesses die gradually. They wonder why they are going through such problems.

Sometimes, one has to look back in retrospect to check whether he is the cause of his problem. I remember the story of the young prophet, who was doing perfectly well until he was deceived and he went back to eat at a wrong place.

"⁴And it came to pass, when king Jeroboam heard the saying of the man of God, which had cried

> *against the altar in Beth–el, that he put forth his hand from the altar, saying, Lay hold on him. In addition, his hand, which he put forth against him, dried up, so that he could not pull it in again to him. ²¹And he cried unto the man of God that came from Judah, saying, Thus saith the LORD, Forasmuch as thou hast disobeyed the mouth of the LORD, and hast not kept the commandment which the LORD thy God commanded thee, ²²But camest back, and hast eaten bread and drunk water in the place, of the which the LORD did say to thee, Eat no bread, and drink no water; thy carcass shall not come unto the sepulcher of thy fathers. ²³And it came to pass, after he had eaten bread, and after he had drunk, that he saddled for him the ass, to wit, for the prophet whom he had brought back. ²⁴And when he was gone, a lion met him by the way, and slew him: and his carcass was cast in the way, and the ass stood by it, the lion also stood by the carcass"* (<u>1 Kings 13:4, 21-24</u>)

Naaman was a great man, a captain of the host of the Syrian army but he was a leper. His original skin was arrested and detained in a far away country. He spent money traveling from one hospital to another. He has delivered many people including his own nation many times but he could not deliver his own skin from the demon of leprosy. He needed help but he could not get it.

> *"Now Naaman, captain of the host of the king of Syria, was a great man with his master, and honorable, because by him the LORD had given deliverance unto Syria: he was also a mighty man in velour, but he was a leper. And the Syrians had gone out by companies, and had brought away captive out of the land of Israel a little*

house cleaner; and she waited on Naaman's wife. And she said unto her mistress, Would God my lord were with the prophet that is in Samaria! For he would recover him of his leprosy. And one went in, and told his lord, saying, thus and thus said the house cleaner that is of the land of Israel. And the king of Syria said, Go to, go, and I will send a letter unto the king of Israel. And he departed, and took with him ten talents of silver, and six thousand pieces of gold, and ten changes of raiment" (2 Kings 5:1-5).

The purpose of this book is to introduce you to the greatest deliverance minister on earth. You need deliverance from poverty, lack and business failures. What you need is information and obedience to a simple instruction and you will recover all your loss.

"And Elisha sent a messenger unto him, saying, Go and wash in Jordan seven times, and thy flesh shall come again to thee, and thou shall be clean. But Naaman was worth, and went away, and said, Behold, I thought, He will surely come out to me, and stand, and call on the name of the LORD his God, and strike his hand over the place, and recover the leper. Are not Abana and Pharpar, rivers of Damascus, better than all the waters of Israel? May I not wash in them, and be clean? Therefore, he turned and went away in a rage. And his servants came near, and spake unto him, and said, My father, if the prophet had bid thee do some great thing, wouldest thou not have done it? How much rather then, when he saith to thee, Wash, and be clean? Then went he down, and dipped himself seven times in Jordan, according to the saying of the man of God: and his flesh came again like unto the flesh of a little child, and he was clean" (2 Kings 5:10-14).

Obedience is better than sacrifice!

It is a matter of decision. If you decide to surrender your life to God or rededicate your life to God, you will recover all your losses and become better than the best. Noah decided to live a righteous life in the midst of corrupt business people. The result was that he found favor before God and in the time of destruction, God spared his life. God will spare your business in times of economic distress. He told Jacob to leave Laban and on his way, He changed his name.

Joseph took a decision not to commit fornication and God made him second in command in the nation of Egypt. Moses decided to stay with God's people and God blessed him and made him a deliverance minister that parted the red sea.

> *"^{24}By faith Moses, when he was come to years, refused to be called the son of Pharaoh's daughter; ^{25}Choosing rather to suffer affliction with the people of God, than to enjoy the pleasures of sin for a season; ^{32}And what shall I more say? for the time would fail me to tell of Gideon, and of Barak, and of Samson, and of Jephthae; of David also, and Samuel, and of the prophets: ^{33}Who through faith subdued kingdoms, wrought righteousness, obtained promises, stopped the mouths of lions, ^{34}Quenched the violence of fire, escaped the edge of the sword, out of weakness were made strong, waxed valiant in fight, turned to flight the armies of the aliens"* (Hebrews 11:24-25, 32-34).

If you believe God today, you will subdue your own kingdom. Your business would be released from all manner of captivity, in the name of Jesus - Amen.

PRAYERS FOR BREAKTHROUGH IN YOUR BUSINESS

Bible reference: <u>Genesis 39:1-6</u>

Begin with praise and worship

1. Father Lord, link me up to the right business You have ordained for me, in the name of Jesus.

2. Let the power of God link me to right people to do business with, in the name of Jesus.

3. Lord Jesus, develop my business ability exceedingly, in the name of Jesus.

4. I receive advancement and growth for my business now, in the name of Jesus.

5. Any strongman that is blocking my progress in business, collapse and die, in the name of Jesus.

6. Holy Ghost fire, burn + remove every hindrance on my way to breakthrough, in the name of Jesus.

7. I use fire to dismantle + bind evil darkness that hovers over my business, in the name of Jesus.

8. Any evil movement against my business, stop and die, in the name of Jesus.

9. I disorganize every failure in business that was organized for me, in the name of Jesus.

10. I uproot evil altars that were built to destroy my businesses with force, in the name of Jesus.

Prayers for breakthrough in your business

11. Any power that is occupying my business in the spiritual world, give up the ghost, in the name of Jesus.

12. Any intimidating force that withstands my business exploits is intimidated to death, in the name of Jesus.

13. You, the ground of my business, become fertile, in the name of Jesus.

14. O Lord, bring my business to the limelight, in the name of Jesus.

15. Any evil altar that has arrested my business, release it by force, in the name of Jesus.

16. Any evil tree that was planted anywhere against my business, I dismantle you from your root, in the name of Jesus.

17. Any evil power that is destroying or harvesting my business efforts, die without mercy, in the name of Jesus.

18. O Lord, arise and give me a business that will advance me greatly, in the name of Jesus.

19. Any evil hand that is reaping good things I sowed in my business, dry up, in the name of Jesus.

20. O Lord, give me divine energy, wisdom and knowledge to do great businesses, in the name of Jesus.

21. Every satanic limitation that was placed upon my business, disappear by force, in the name of Jesus.

My Kan is a kingdom advancer!

22. I command every demonic activity that is going on against my business to die, in the name of Jesus.

23. I oppose witches or wizards that re attacking my businesses, in the name of Jesus.

24. I reject every dream that was designed to destroy my business, in the name of Jesus.

25. Enemies of my efforts in life are wasted by fire, in the name of Jesus.

26. Any oppression that is going on against my business is terminated by force, in the name of Jesus.

27. I receive the anointing to prosper exceedingly in my business, in the name of Jesus.

28. O Lord, grant me favor to experience a business breakthrough, in the name of Jesus.

29. Any frustration that is targeting my businesses is terminated by force, in the name of Jesus.

30. Let satanic money and evil seeds that were planted to destroy my business die, in the name of Jesus.

31. Every enemy of God's will in my business, die, in the name of Jesus.

32. I terminate every evil control going on in my businesses, in the name of Jesus.

33. Every instrument of business failure in my life is roasted by fire, in the name of Jesus.

34. Every good thing that has abandoned my business, come back now, in the name of Jesus.

35. I disgrace agents of devil that were planted to destroy my business, in the name of Jesus.

36. Let evil forces against my business be removed by the power of God, in the name of Jesus.

37. Any satanic door that was opened to my business, close forever, in the name of Jesus.

38. I withdraw my business from evil contacts, in the name of Jesus.

39. Let evil priests that are ministering in my business go blind, in the name of Jesus.

40. Let bad legs that have walked into my business walk out by force, in the name of Jesus.

41. Every spirit of failure that was programmed into my business, I cast you out now, in the name of Jesus.

42. Every enemy of my business breakthroughs is arrested to death, in the name of Jesus.

43. O Lord, deliver my businesses from the hands of evil people, in the name of Jesus.

44. O Lord, command financial prosperity to overtake my business, in the name of Jesus.

45. Let evil powers that have vowed to stop my breakthrough in business die immediately, in the name of Jesus.

46. O Lord, prosper my business forever, in the name of Jesus.

Prayers for breakthrough in your business

47. Every messenger of failure to my business, carry your message to your sender, in the name of Jesus.

48. Let any evil plan to destroy my business scatter, in the name of Jesus.

49. Let every opportunity my business has lost come back immediately, in the name of Jesus.

50. Any graveyard that has buried my business, vomit it immediately, in the name of Jesus.

51. Let evil stones that are holding my business to a halt roll away now, in the name of Jesus.

52. Let evil covenant or curse that is frustrating my business break and expire, in the name of Jesus.

53. Any pollution and defilement that exists in my business, receive cleansing now, in the name of Jesus.

54. Blood of Jesus, deliver my business from death, in the name of Jesus.

55. I arrest evil forces that are fighting my business, in the name of Jesus.

56. I convert every defeat my business has ever suffered to victory, in the name of Jesus.

57. Let any witchcraft animal that is scattering my business die immediately, in the name of Jesus.

58. Every enemy of my breakthrough in business is disgrace, in the name of Jesus.

59. O Lord, arise and take my business to the top, in the name of Jesus.

60. You, my business, wake up from sleep and prosper exceedingly, in the name of Jesus.

Thank You So Much!

Beloved, I hope you enjoyed this book as much as I believe God has touched your heart today. I cannot thank you enough for your continued support for this prayer ministry.

I appreciate you so much for taking out time to read this wonderful prayer book, and if you have an extra second, I would love to hear what you think about this book.

Please, do share your testimonies with me by sending emails to pastor@prayermadueke.com, or through the social media at www.facebook.com/prayer.madueke. I invite you also to www.prayermadueke.com to view other books I have written on various issues of life, especially on marriage, family, sexual problems and money.

I will be delighted to partner with you in organized crusades, ceremonies, marriages and Marriage seminars, special events, church ministration and fellowship for the advancement of God's Kingdom here on earth.

Thank you again, and I wish you success in your life.

God bless you.

In Christ,

Prayer M. Madueke

OTHER BOOKS BY PRAYER M. MADUEKE

- *21/40 Nights Of Decrees And Your Enemies Will Surrender*
- *Confront And Conquer*
- *Tears in Prison*
- *35 Special Dangerous Decrees*
- *The Reality of Spirit Marriage*
- *Queen of Heaven*
- *Leviathan the Beast*
- *100 Days Prayer To Wake Up Your Lazarus*
- *Dangerous Decrees To Destroy Your Destroyers*
- *The spirit of Christmas*
- *More Kingdoms To Conquer*
- *Your Dream Directory*
- *The Sword Of New Testament Deliverance*
- *Alphabetic Battle For Unmerited Favors*
- *Alphabetic Character Deliverance*
- *Holiness*
- *The Witchcraft Of The Woman That Sits Upon Many Waters*
- *The Operations Of The Woman That Sits Upon Many Waters*
- *Powers To Pray Once And Receive Answers*
- *Prayer Riots To Overthrow Divorce*
- *Prayers To Get Married Happily*
- *Prayers To Keep Your Marriage Out of Troubles*
- *Prayers For Conception And Power To Retain*
- *Prayer Retreat – Prayers to Possess Your Year*
- *Prayers for Nation Building*
- *Organized student in a disorganized school*
- *Welcome to Campus*
- *Alone with God (10 series)*

Prayers for breakthrough in your business

CONTACTS

AFRICA
#1 Babatunde close,
Off Olaitan Street, Surulere
Lagos, Nigeria
+234 803 353 0599
pastor@prayermadueke.com

#Plot 1791, No. 3 Ijero Close,
Flat 2, Area 1,
Garki 1 - FCT, Abuja
+234 807 065 4159

IRELAND
Ps Emmanuel Oko
#84 Thornfield Square
Cloudalkin D22
Ireland
Tel: +353 872 820 909, +353 872 977 422
aghaoko2003@yahoo.com

EUROPE/SCHENGEN
Collins Kwame
#46 Felton Road
Barking
Essex IG11 7XZ GB
Tel: +44 208 507 8083, +44 787 703 2386, +44 780 703 6916
aghaoko2003@yahoo.com

Made in United States
Troutdale, OR
12/13/2024

26369703R00022